Making Music

Mick Gowar and Simon Gunton

OXFORD
UNIVERSITY PRESS

OXFORD
UNIVERSITY PRESS

Great Clarendon Street, Oxford OX2 6DP

Oxford University Press is a department of the University of Oxford.
It furthers the University's objective of excellence in research, scholarship,
and education by publishing worldwide in

Oxford   New York

Auckland   Cape Town   Dar es Salaam   Hong Kong   Karachi
Kuala Lumpur   Madrid   Melbourne   Mexico City   Nairobi
New Delhi   Shanghai   Taipei   Toronto

With offices in

Argentina   Austria   Brazil   Chile   Czech Republic   France   Greece
Guatemala   Hungary   Italy   Japan   Poland   Portugal   Singapore
South Korea   Switzerland   Thailand   Turkey   Ukraine   Vietnam

Oxford is a registered trade mark of Oxford University Press
in the UK and in certain other countries

British Library Cataloguing in Publication Data

Data available

ISBN 978-0-19-919871-9

10

Printed in China by Imago

Paper used in the production of this book is a natural,
recyclable product made from wood grown in sustainable forests.
The manufacturing process conforms to the environmental
regulations of the country of origin.

Acknowledgements

The publisher would like to thank the following for permission to reproduce
photographs: **p4** Simon Gunton/Mick Gowar, **p5**t Simon Gunton/Mick Gowar, b OUP, **p6** Simon
Gunton/Mick Gowar, **p7** Simon Gunton/Mick Gowar, **p8**r Corbis/Richard T Nowitz,
l Ancient Art & Architecture, **p9**b Ancient Art & Architecture, t Bridgeman Art Library/Leeds
Museums & Galleries, **p10** Simon Gunton/Mick Gowar, **p12** Corbis/McPherson Colin/Sygma, **p14**
Simon Gunton/Mick Gowar, **p15** OUP, **p16** Simon Gunton/Mick Gowar, **p17** Kobal/Universal,
p18 Dominic Photography, **p19** Arenaimages, **p20** OUP, **p21** Simon Gunton/Mick Gowar, **pp22**,
23, **24** Simon Gunton/Mick Gowar, **p25** Corbis/Historical Picture Archive, **p26** Simon
Gunton/Mick Gowar, **p27**t Simon Gunton/Mick Gowar, b Getty Images/Don Bonsey, **p29**t
Alice Arnold, b Alamy/Lesley Garland Picture Library

Cover: Penny Brown

Illustrations by David Russell: **p6**, **p8**; Stefan Chabluk: **p12**t; Martin Aston: **p12**b, **p30**

Contents

Music Maker

Simon Says

Hi, my name's Simon Gunton.
I'm a professional musician. I play the
trombone, the bass trumpet and,
occasionally, a very old instrument called
a sackbut. I can also play the piano.

I've played the trombone with
all the major London orchestras.
I've also played in brass bands,
with pop groups and as a soloist
– playing concerts on my own,
or just with a pianist.

Did you know?

The earliest trombones were called
sackbuts. This name comes from the
old French name for the instrument:
saqueboute, which means pull-push.

I belong to a small group called *Story Force*, and we go to schools all over the country to help children compose and perform their own musical shows, often based on traditional stories. We've done shows based on creepy stories about goblins and ghosts, and one about the great Saxon hero, Beowulf, who fights monsters and kills dragons.

The group is called *Story Force*, because like the TV gardening programme *Ground Force*, we guarantee a great result in only a few days!

I've played the music for films, some of which you may have seen. I've also played on many rock and pop records. You've probably heard me play – but you didn't know it was me!

Brass instruments

Brass instruments, like Simon's, are played by the musician blowing through a mouth piece into a length of metal tubing.

The pitch of the note – whether it is high or low – depends on the length of the tube. The longer the tube, the lower the sound. To play more notes – higher or lower – the player has to alter the length of the tube the sound is going through.

hunting horn

euphonium

Horns

Simple horns like hunting horns can only play a small number of notes. But modern brass instruments like the trumpet, the tuba and the euphonium can play more notes than a hunting horn. They have valves which open and close sections of the instrument's tubing. This alters the length of the tube the sound is going through, so the player can play more notes.

The simplest way of altering the length of the tube is found in the trombone. Part of the tubing – called the slide – moves in and out. The length of the tube I blow through increases when the slide is pushed out and decreases when it's pulled in. So I can play higher notes when the slide is pulled up, and lower notes when the slide is pushed out.

trombone

Ancient brass

Paintings found in tombs show that most types of musical instrument we know today – plucked strings, drums, blown instruments – were played in ancient Egypt.

Did you know?

One of the oldest instruments still in use is the Jewish shofar. It's made from a ram's horn. The shofar is blown during the festival of *Rosh Hashanah*, the Jewish New Year, which celebrates the creation of the world.

A tomb painting showing Egyptian musicians playing guitar-like instruments.

Simon Says

In the Bible you can find several stories about the power of ancient instruments – especially instruments like horns and trumpets. One of the most famous stories is about the Israelite General Joshua. His army was besieging the city of Jericho.

He commanded the trumpet players in his army to march round and round the city blowing their instruments, and the huge sound they made caused the walls of Jericho to crack and fall down.

The Scots Greys charging at the battle of Waterloo. Bugle calls were essential for commanding calvalry.

Joshua's trumpeters bringing down the walls of Jericho.

Did you know?

A trumpet or bugle can be heard above the noise of cannon fire and gunshots. Before radio was invented, a bugle- or trumpet-call was a good way for an army general to signal to his troops when he wanted them to advance, retreat or attack.

The best known army bugle call is The Last Post, which is still played in army camps at the end of the day. It is also played at military funerals and Remembrance Day services.

Becoming a musician

"Simon Says"

I started playing the trombone when I was very young. The first band I joined was the Salvation Army band. You've probably seen a Salvation Army band playing carols at Christmas time, to raise money to help homeless people.

I joined the local Junior Band when I was nine and played with the Salvation Army until I was 18 and left home to go to music college in London. It was playing in the Salvation Army Junior Band that got me really hooked on playing music.

But as you'll see in this book, I've always loved playing lots of different sorts of music. So, when I was 16 I auditioned to play for an orchestra: the Leicestershire Schools Symphony Orchestra.

I was really nervous at the audition. I played some very difficult scales and a piece I'd worked on with my trombone teacher – to show I was good enough to join. Luckily for me they thought I was!

It was fantastic playing in the orchestra. I made life-long friends, and I was playing great music with great people!

One of the best things was that every Christmas, Easter and summer holidays we had special courses. All the members of the orchestra went away together – like going on a school camp or holiday. It was great fun, and we got to study with really top professional musicians.

We played the sort of pieces that a professional orchestra would play – concertos and symphonies by composers like *Beethoven, Mozart* and *Mahler* (see page 32). And we were treated like professional musicians, too – we even went on foreign tours. It was great fun, and fabulous training for when I started to play in professional orchestras.

Did you know?

There are youth orchestras or schools orchestras in most counties and in a lot of big towns and cities. If you want to find out more, you can ask the music teacher at your school, or ask at your local library.

Rehearsing and performing

This is the programme for a traditional 'classical' concert.

TUE 26 OCT 2004, 7:30 PM
ROYAL FESTIVAL HALL

Royal Philharmonic Orchestra
Series: Royal Philharmonic Orchestra 2004/05

Richard Wagner Overture,
Der fliegende Hollander

Ludwig Van Beethoven Piano
Concerto No.5 in E flat (Emperor)

INTERVAL

Edward Elgar Enigma Variations

Royal Philharmonic Orchestra

Garry Walker conductor

Paul Lewis piano

"Simon Says"

There's no time to learn the notes you're going to play in rehearsal. Every musician in an orchestra must be able to play, perfectly, whatever is put on their music stand. Rehearsals are for the conductor to explain *how* they want the orchestra to play the pieces.

Did you know?

Professional musicians in an orchestra have to be able to play a whole programme like this with maybe only one rehearsal!

The Conductor

The conductor's first job is to study the music and decide things like how fast the musicians should play, how loudly, and when there should be pauses in the music. These things often aren't clear from the music the composer has written. Then the conductor has to communicate their ideas to the orchestra.

In rehearsals, the conductor can stop the orchestra and ask them to play louder, softer, faster or slower. But that can't happen during a performance. During the concert, the conductor only has a baton or their hands to signal these things to the orchestra.

Simon Says

Are you fit enough to be a conductor?

Try this:

● Hold your arms out straight ahead, slightly above shoulder height

● Now, keeping your arms straight, move them vigorously from side to side.

I guarantee that your arms will start aching, and you'll want to stop within a few minutes.

Did you know?

If you were conducting *Das Rheingold*, the first part of *Wagner's Ring* cycle of operas, you would have to do that for nearly three hours – without a break!

Movie music

British musicians are famous throughout the world for being the best at sight-reading – that means being able to play music they've never seen before, perfectly, as soon as it's put in front of them. That's why so many Hollywood producers choose British orchestras to record the music for their films – because British musicians do a superb job.

An orchestra recording a film soundtrack.

Shrek, Shrek 2, Beauty and The Beast, Shark Tale, Charlie and the Chocolate Factory and *The Lord of The Rings* are some of the film soundtracks I've played on. Although I've recorded a lot, my favourite one was playing on the soundtrack of a James Bond film. That was a real thrill. The first time I played that famous theme – having heard it so many times in the cinema or on TV – was a real spine-tingling moment!

In the earliest days of cinema, when films were silent, music was provided by live musicians. In small cinemas the music was played by a solo pianist or organist, but in the biggest cinemas in London, New York or Paris there was a band or small orchestra to play.

Most films had no written music at all. The pianist or organist in a small cinema had to improvise music to fit what was happening on the screen – as it was happening!

Because there were no sound effects or speech in these early films, music was very important to express things like the personalities of the characters, their emotions, and the general mood of a film or scene.

Film and TV music does much the same job today as the earliest film music – reflecting the feelings of the characters and what is happening in each scene. The difference is that the music for a modern film or TV play is written by a highly skilled composer who specialises in writing music that can fit a scene in a film or TV programme to within a fraction of a second.

Really good film music can make a film feel much more exciting and mysterious – like the swirling, magical, flying music from the Harry Potter films. It can also make a film feel scary, like the sinister shark music from Jaws, which gets louder and louder, and faster and faster, to sound like a shark that is getting closer and closer!

Opera and theatre music

Some operas need almost as many special effects as a feature film. *Wagner's Ring*, for example, needs a dragon, mermaids swimming through water, and in the last scene the heroine rides her horse into a funeral pyre!

The orchestra in a theatre or opera house is normally in a 'pit' – a sunken area in front of the stage. So when I'm playing in an opera, usually I can't see what's happening on stage. The musicians in an opera orchestra have to watch the conductor very carefully, because only the conductor can see what's going on and can direct the music to match the action on stage.

Sometimes I get the chance to appear on stage in an opera. If there's a character in the opera who has to play music on stage, I might get the chance to act! In *Lady Macbeth of Mstensk*, an opera by the Russian composer Dimitri Shostakovich, I played three parts. I even had a dresser to help me with the costume changes. It was great to share in the action of the opera as well as helping to make the music.

Musicals

Maybe it's because of the popularity of action and adventure films that audiences look for amazing special effects when they come to see musical plays.

Rock 'n' roll trombone!

Many pop bands are either all vocal groups, or have the standard pop group line-up: guitar-bass-drums. So when it comes to recording, and sometimes performing as well, they need to find musicians to play the other instruments.

Did you know?

It's very common for pop groups and singers to use brass players to add to their sound.

Simon Says

I've made a lot of pop records. I've recorded for Paul McCartney, Missy Elliot, Elton John, George Michael, Robbie Williams, Delta Goodrem, Brian McFadden and Westlife. But with modern recording techniques, you don't necessarily get to meet the stars. Often the session musicians record the backing track, then several days later the star artists record the vocals in a studio, sometimes thousands of miles away.

Some of the CDs Simon has played on.

Simon (left) inside Abbey Road Studios, where some of the most famous pop stars in the world have recorded their songs.

"Simon Says"

One of my first recording sessions was with a singer called Arrow. We recorded a single called *Hot, Hot, Hot* which got into the Top Ten.

I was invited to join Arrow's touring band in 1984, and I played with them for six years. It was a real multi-national band. I was the only English member. The other musicians came from Africa, the Caribbean, the US and Australia.

We played concerts all over the UK, Europe and America – and I was on *Top of the Pops*!

Chamber music

The 'classical' music equivalent of a pop group is a chamber music group.

The name 'chamber music' simply means 'room music' – music to be played in normal sized rooms rather than concert halls or theatres.

Simon (far left) rehearsing with an early music chamber group, The Gabrielli Players.

"Simon Says"

I belong to a brass chamber group called *The Golden Section*. It's a brass quintet consisting of two trumpeters, a tuba player, a French horn player, and me playing trombone. For some shows we bring in other musicians – often drummers and percussionists.

It's not a very common combination of instruments, but over the last twenty years a lot of new pieces have been written for a brass quintet. We've also commissioned new pieces – that means we've asked composers to write pieces specially for us to play. That can be really exciting – playing a piece that no one has ever played or heard before.

Music for everyone

All the big orchestras, and many other groups, run special projects in schools, hospitals and other places to bring music – and the fun of music-making – to people who might not otherwise get the opportunity to try it.

Simon's latest project

At the moment, I'm working on a big project in Cambridge. I'm working with adults who are in hospitals and care homes. They aren't musicians or composers, but I'm helping them to make up a series of pieces of music, with words, all about the city they live in.

When the whole piece is finished, we'll be performing it in King's College Chapel – from where the famous Christmas carol service is broadcast on Christmas Eve. It'll be a great experience for the patients, and their families, to hear their music and words performed by professional musicians in a world famous venue.

King's College Chapel

Composing

The beginning of the twenty-first century is a great time to be a composer. There are so many types of music to write and learn from – like rock, pop and jazz – which didn't exist a hundred years ago.

There are also many more opportunities for composers to write music than there were in the past. Films, TV programmes and advertisements all need music. And, of course, orchestras, chamber groups and solo musicians need new, exciting and challenging music to play.

Did you know?

Instruments like software synthesizers and samplers, which today's composers use, didn't even exist twenty years ago.

Simon's studio in his house.

This is my studio. It's the special room in my house where I compose and record music. I compose lots of different types of music. I've written pop songs and music for adverts. I wrote music for a TV series called *The Cazalets*, a drama series about a family living in Britain at the beginning of the Second World War, which was shown on British and American television.

I also wrote some scary music for a fantasy series about a creepy family who live in a terrifying castle, called *Gormenghast*.

The castle of Gormenghast

Music and technology

Like a lot of today's composers, Simon uses a computer programme called *Sibelius* to help him.

Simon Says

It's not the sort of programme which gives you tunes or samples. You have to type in the notes, but then it can play back what you've written with all the sounds of the different instruments.

With *Sibelius* I can write a really big concert piece and get a good idea of what it will sound like played by all the instruments of the orchestra.

I also use the computer for making recordings – including recordings of the pieces children have written on education projects like *Story Force*.

Did you know?

By using computers, composers can now make music out of all sorts of different sounds. They can mix all kinds of recorded sounds with music played by orchestral musicians.

One of the best examples of this is *City Life* by Steve Reich. It's a 'sound picture' of life in New York City, and it mixes together the voice of someone trying to sell umbrellas, the noise of road drills and hammers on a building site, and the sound of car horns with brilliant instrumental writing.

Steve Reich

Have a go!

Computer technology and the Internet offer musicians of all ages lots of new opportunities for making and sharing their music.

Simon Says

There's a great BBC Radio 3 website for children called *Making Tracks*.

The website has got everything you need – like easy composition programmes – to help you start making your own music. And there's a special website where you can share your compositions with others.

Making Tracks also has a weekly top ten of the best tracks that children have sent in. Have a go! It might be the start of your career in music!

Glossary

audition – a job interview for a musician or performer, in which they demonstrate what they can do. A musician auditioning for an orchestra might play several short pieces

besiege – to surround an enemy to make them surrender

Chitty-Chitty-Bang-Bang – a film and stage show based on the novel for children by Ian Fleming about an eccentric inventor called Caractacus Potts who repairs an old car to amuse his children. The car can do things no ordinary car can do, like fly. The wicked Baron Bomburst tries to kidnap Caractacus and steal the car so he can win the British Grand Prix

cliché – an idea or a phrase which has been so overused that it has become a kind of joke, e.g. 'good as gold' and 'truth is stranger than fiction'

concerto – a long piece of concert music played by an orchestra and a solo instrument. It is usually divided into different sections known as movements

Remembrance Day – a day on which people remember soldiers who were killed in the First, Second World Wars and later wars

Salvation Army – the Salvation Army is a Christian church which is well known for helping homeless people, alcoholics and drug addicts. It is also famous for its brass bands, which are often heard in town centres at Christmas time playing carols and collecting money to help them in their social work

Sibelius – music-writing software, named after the Finnish composer Jean Sibelius. Sibelius also makes software to help people who are just learning to play instruments or learn about music

symphony – a long and complicated piece of music divided into three or more movements. A symphony orchestra is a large orchestra made up of brass, woodwind, string and percussion instruments

Musical composers

Wolfgang Amadeus Mozart

Austrian composer, born 1756, died 1791. He is believed by many people to be the greatest composer who ever lived. Mozart was a child genius, both as a performer and a composer. He gave his first concerts when he was six, and his first compositions were published when he was 8. As an adult he seemed to be able to compose any form of music brilliantly – operas, concerts, chamber music, so maybe it is not surprising that when he died, there was a rumour that Mozart had been murdered by a rival composer who was jealous of him.

Ludwig van Beethoven

German composer, born 1770, died 1827. Beethoven wrote symphonies about his life, his opinions and his fears. By the time he was 50, Beethoven was totally deaf; however, this didn't stop him composing. Wherever he went he took notebooks in which he wrote hundreds of tunes and musical ideas.

Richard Wagner

German composer, born 1813, died 1883. Wagner was fascinated by old legends and myths. He composed operas, many of them extremely long, based on myths and legends. *The Ring* is a series of four operas based on old German and Norse legends of gods, mortals, dwarfs and giants fighting each other to possess a magic ring which will make them rulers of the world. Not only did Wagner write the music for his operas, he also wrote all the words and built his own theatre to stage them.

Gustav Mahler

Austrian composer and conductor, born 1860, died 1911. A great conductor of concert music and operas, Mahler was one of the greatest composers of symphonies. He wrote eleven symphonies, including a symphony of songs called *The Song of The Earth*. Mahler liked to compose for enormous orchestras. His 8th symphony needs over 1000 performers, including an orchestra and a choir!

Dimitri Shostakovich

Russian composer, born 1906, died 1975. He composed symphonies, piano works, songs, operas and film music. Shostakovich offended the Soviet dictator Josef Stalin and was in great danger until Stalin's death in 1952.

Steve Reich

American composer, born 1936. Steve Reich is famous for composing music using recordings of people speaking and samples of sounds from the environment, as well as orchestral instruments. He has composed music using the smallest number of people or the simplest instruments – for example, *Clapping Music* for two performers clapping.